TEX-MEX
FROM SCRATCH

BY: Jonas Cramby
PHOTOGRAPHY BY: Roland Persson

STERLING EPICURE
New York

CONTENTS

Left: Beef chili taco (p. 70)

TEX-MEX
FROM SCRATCH

My name is Jonas Cramby, and I'm addicted to tacos. I love Tex-Mex food so much that I named my eldest daughter Dixie as her first name and Margarita as her middle name, and my youngest daughter Lone Star (after the nickname for the state of Texas). And if I ever have a third, she'll be named Carnita—after my favorite taco filling (recipe on p. 78).

And just to make things clear here, we're not talking about that kind of horrible Mexican food available from fast-food chains or TV dinners, nor are we talking about bordering-on-racist Tex-Mex parties with Tequila Slammers, fake moustaches, and "funny" sombreros, or Friday nights in with hard taco shells that break up and fall all over your knee after the first bite. This book is about really tasty, homemade Tex-Mex grub made from scratch.

Although the word "Tex-Mex" has carried a negative connotation for a long time, it's about as intelligent to reject a whole cuisine on these grounds as to say they have bad food in Italy because you can also get spaghetti and meatballs in a can.

Real Tex-Mex is, like so many other good things, the result of a culture clash. German immigrants brought their smoky sausages and creamy potato salads to Texas, and these food traditions soon merged with the cowboys' simple prairie grub and the Mexicans' beautiful food culture—which in turn was a fusion between the Spanish and Native American cuisines. The result became simple food that is easy to like and that makes you happy.

More and more people seem to be understanding this. The word "taco" is nowadays the most frequent search term on recipe sites, and Mexican grub is experiencing a revival. Many hip young American restaurateurs have left their restaurants to start mobile food purveyors in so-called taco trucks. Mexican inspiration is also noticeable in American fine dining, with chef Rick Bayless in the forefront, and in Texas the long-despised Tex-Mex

cuisine, eagerly egged on by food journalist Robb Walsh, has become re-evaluated and is now seen as a proud part of the state's cultural heritage.

It's from the states bordering Mexico in general and from Texas in particular that I have gathered inspiration for this cookbook.

It all began about 12 years ago when I went for my first road trip through the United States. When I reached the states on the border with Mexico, I soon started to notice all the small, ramshackle street-food joints and rusty taco trucks, which had colorful signs boldly stating that here I would find *tacos ricos* (delicious tacos), *tacos los mejores del mundo* (the best tacos in the world) or *tacos superfantasticos* (as it sounds).

That such good food could be cooked in hovels felt a little like bragging to me. But the thing was, it was true, almost all these places actually served the world's best Tex-Mex grub. For only a

"Tex-Mex is simple food that is easy to like and that makes you happy."

few dollars I could get a pile of mesquite-grilled meat, served in a soft, warm home-baked wheat tortilla with grilled salad, onion, and a couple of big crispy radishes on top—then a twist of lime and a big spoonful of smoky hot homemade salsa to finish it off. Or why not carnitas? Slow-cooked, sweet-spicy pork with a small bowl on the side filled with the frying juices for dipping. Or a plateful of barbecued pork or beef: smoky, tender, and sticky, served on a piece of paper with only a couple of crackers and a Mexican beer, so cold that your front teeth could almost crack.

When I came back home, I missed these places like you miss an old friend. So I soon made sure that more and more work trips and vacations took me to the states bordering Mexico, and after a while I also started to put my head into the kitchens and ask for the recipes. When I returned home, I started to experiment, refine, and adjust the cooking processes to my home conditions and realized that you actually could, with a minimal amount of effort, cook the world's best everyday food at home.

In this book, I will teach you just that. I will go through the basics as well as more advanced dishes. I will gather inspiration from both sides of the border, and it will include parts from each section of the Tex-Mex cuisine's food circle—crispy, hot, sweet, sour, and sticky. But above all, it will be *superfantastico*.

Jonas Cramby

PART 1

BASICS

The first thing you need to know about cooking Tex-Mex food is that it's fun and colorful with a huge amount of flavor. So be generous with the lime and chili. The second thing is: no cans, jars, or plastic packages can be used. Here, we always do everything from scratch.

TORTILLAS AND BURGER BUNS

If you want to start making your own tortilla bread, you need to know that there are two different kinds: wheat and corn. The Mexican corn tortilla tastes delicious and, well, corny—but only in its literal sense—while the wheat tortilla is a little smoother, breadier, and softer. The wheat variety is also the traditional Tex-Mex tortilla and is used for tacos and when larger bread is needed; for example, when making enchiladas and burritos.

Homemade wheat tortillas

If you absolutely have to, you can use store-bought tortillas that you heat up in the oven. They are okay. But if you really want to impress, you should, of course, make your own. It's a lot easier than you think.

About 16 large (8 inches/20cm)
or 30 small (4 inches/10cm)
11¼ cups/3lb 2oz/1.4kg all-purpose flour
1 teaspoon baking powder
1 teaspoon salt
4 tablespoons butter
2½ cups/1 pint/600ml warm water

Mix the flour, baking powder, and salt together in a bowl. Dice the butter into small cubes and add to the flour mix. Slowly pour the warm water over the flour-and-butter mixture. Mix together to a sticky dough. Knead on a floured work surface for about 2 minutes, put it back into the bowl, and cover with damp paper towels. Let rest for 20 minutes. Once the dough has rested, divide into 16 or 30 portions and roll into small balls. Roll out the balls to round tortilla disks. Let rest for 10 minutes. Cook the disks in a dry skillet for about 30 seconds on each side and serve them *à la minute* if you want to be fancy. Alternatively, preheat the oven to 210°F/100°C and reheat them just before serving, preferably wrapped in a towel or in a tortilla warmer. If you'd like those fancy grill stripes, you can also fry them in a ridged grill pan.

Homemade corn tortillas

Corn tortillas are a little trickier than the wheat variety—but also tastier if you get it right. Remember they have to be eaten immediately. With wheat tortillas, you can prepare them a couple of hours in advance and then reheat, while corn tortillas start tasting like Play-Doh after only half an hour—although day-old corn tortillas are the ones to use if you want to make your own nachos, crispy tacos, or tostadas. Just deep-fry, drain on paper towels, and season with salt. Delicious! You do, however, need some special ingredients and equipment:

MASA HARINA (CORN FLOUR)

Masa harina is a corn flour made from corn kernels that have been treated with slaked lime before being ground. To use, just mix with water and salt. It cannot be replaced by ordinary cornstarch or anything else—the only alternative in that case is to produce your own masa harina, but then you need Maíz Pozolero and slaked lime, so let's not bother right now. Several varieties of masa harina corn flour (made with yellow, white, or blue corn) are available in some large supermarkets, Latin American food stores, specialty delis, and online.

TORTILLA PRESS

Because the dough made with masa harina is delicate and crumbly, you need a tortilla press if you want to make your own corn tortillas. If you do have one of these, it's really easy (and fun). You can either make your own tortilla press or buy one in a store or online.

TORTILLA WARMER

You can use dish towels to keep your tortillas warm, but if you take your Tex-Mex food seriously, you'll get a much better result with a proper tortilla warmer. The corn tortilla softens perfectly and will keep warm for hours. It is available from some larger supermarkets or department stores and online.

Once you've got all the equipment, it's easy. Just mix the flour with water and salt according to the directions on the package, mix to a dough, and roll into balls of an equal size. Place some damp paper towels on top so that the balls don't dry out. Place the first ball in the tortilla press—which you'll have covered in plastic wrap or a plastic bag so that the dough doesn't get stuck—and press down. Be assertive, but don't go nuts and whack it like it's an amusement park attraction. Lift up the press and, *voilà!*, there it is. Your first corn tortilla.

Remember that the rounder you make the ball, the rounder the tortilla will be. Cook your tortillas in a dry, medium-warm nonstick skillet. When they're done, they are hard and don't seem particularly tasty—that's when you put them into your tortilla warmer, where they keep warm for ages and turn nice and soft.

Homemade tortilla chips

I promise, once you've started making your own tortilla chips, you will never eat those sad excuses you can buy from the store again. There's just one problem: You have to make them from real corn tortillas—preferably prepared ones from a Latin American food store, specialty deli, restaurant, or ordered online. Don't worry if they're dry; the result will actually be better if they are. The reason for making the chips using store-bought tortillas is because those you make yourself won't be thin enough to achieve maximum crispiness. And you should absolutely not use wheat tortillas; it won't just turn them worse but will make them outright inedible.

real corn tortillas
oil, for deep-frying
salt

Heat the oil in a deep saucepan to about 350°F/180°C and slice the tortilla into quarters. Deep-fry a couple at a time until golden yellow but not brown, and drain on paper towels. Season with salt and serve with guacamole or a homemade salsa.

Homemade burger buns

An extremely fluffy and soft bun that at the same time can stand up to some meat juice is crucial for a tasty hamburger. Today, there is simply no commercial hamburger bun that is suitable. But how about bread from the bakers? Well, most of them are too wrapped up in their world of flavor-rich sourdough bread with a good crust to realize that some bread should neither taste too much nor offer too much chewiness.

About 12 buns

¼ cup/2fl oz/60ml instant mash potatoes
1¼ cups/10fl oz/300ml milk
2¼ teaspoons active dry yeast
2 tablespoons granulated sugar
1 teaspoon salt
4¾ cups/1¼lb/600g white bread flour
1 egg
4 tablespoons butter, melted

Bring ¾ cup plus 2 tablespoons/ 7fl oz/200ml water to a boil and whisk in the instant mashed potatoes. Heat the milk to 98.6°F/37°C, put the yeast into a bowl, add the milk, and stir until the yeast has dissolved. Add the sugar, salt, and instant mashed potatoes and stir. Add the flour and work the dough in a food processor until smooth. Add the egg and mix a little longer. Pour the melted butter over the mix and continue to work the dough until you have a smooth, fairly loose dough. Let rise for 1 hour. With damp hands, shape the dough into 12 round buns and place on a piece of parchment paper. Let rise for 1 hour without covering.

   Preheat the oven to 400°F/200°C. When the buns have risen, spray with water, place in the oven with a dish filled with water underneath, and bake for about 15 minutes or until they've turned a good color. Remove the buns from the oven, spray them with water again, and cover with a dish towel. Once cooled, remove from the parchment paper, put them in a plastic bag, and seal. This will make the buns turn even softer. While you're at it, take the opportunity to make a large batch; they're perfect for freezing.

Brioche-style burger buns

Fine-dining burgers are often served in a brioche bun.

About 8 buns

1 cup/9fl oz/250ml tepid water
3 tablespoons tepid milk
2 teaspoons active dry yeast
2½ tablespoons granulated sugar
2 extra-large eggs
6 cups/1lb 10oz/750g all-purpose flour
2½ tablespoons butter
1½ teaspoons salt
sesame seeds (optional)

Mix together the water, milk, yeast, and sugar. Let stand for 10 minutes. Meanwhile, whisk 1 egg until fluffy. In a large bowl, mix the flour and butter with your hands, as you would do with a pastry dough. Stir in the yeast mixture, salt, and the whisked egg until a dough appears as if by magic. This dough you will then knead—either by hand or in a food processor—for 8–10 minutes. It will be a little stickier than a normal dough, but that's okay. Shape into a ball, cover with a dish towel, and let rise for 1–2 hours. Divide the ball into 8 portions, then roll them into small, round, fine balls. Place on a baking sheet lined with parchment paper and let rise under the towel for another 1–2 hours.

   Preheat the oven to 400°F/200°C, and place a dish filled with water at the bottom of the oven. Whisk the other egg together with 1 teaspoon of water and brush over the buns. If you'd like a darker color, like in the picture, you can also try adding 1–2 teaspoons baking soda. Sprinkle with the sesame seeds (if you want) and bake for about 15 minutes, until the buns are golden brown. Let cool for a moment before gobbling them up. It's difficult, but otherwise you'll burn your mouth.

GUACAMOLE

Guacamole makes you happy, and that's that. It's hard to think about diseases, aging, and death if you have a frosty mango margarita in your hand and a bowl of newly fried tortilla chips and some guacamole on the table. So don't cheat and get the store-bought stuff—make it from scratch.

Chunky guacamole

This guacamole should be chunky, so you absolutely may not put the avocado in a blender; if you do, you're lazy and might just as well go and buy takeout.

Serves 4
8 avocados
¼ cup/2fl oz/60ml freshly squeezed lime juice
2 tablespoons salt
4–6 garlic cloves, chopped
1 small bunch of fresh cilantro
4 fresh red or green chilis, such as jalapeño or medium-hot chilis
⅔ cup/5fl oz/150ml pico de gallo (see p. 26)

Mash the avocados using a mortar and pestle. Add the lime juice, salt, chopped garlic, cilantro, and chilis. Taste and adjust the seasoning, if needed. Then add a little of the pico de gallo and taste again, with the help of a tortilla chip. If you are unsure about how much of each ingredient to use, note that the heat from the chili should be balanced with the acidity of the lime and the saltiness of the salt.

Guacamole típico

This Mexican everyday "guaca" is more similar to an avocado salad than to the green cream that we associate to when hearing the word "guacamole." The trick is to get the chili paste to cover every little piece of the avocado so that at first it's hot and salty and then smooth and soft.

Serves 2
2 teaspoons finely chopped white onion
1 tablespoon finely chopped fresh chili, such as jalapeño or red/green chili
1 tablespoon finely chopped garlic
½ teaspoon salt
4 cups/7oz/200g fresh cilantro
2 avocados
1–2 tablespoons freshly squeezed lime juice

Mash the onion, chili, garlic, salt, and half of the cilantro to a fine paste using a mortar and pestle. Dice the avocados, squeeze some lime juice over them, and stir into the mashed dressing so that all the pieces are covered. Garnish with the rest of the cilantro.

How much?

If you are unsure about how much guacamole to make, it's better to do too much than too little. You cannot make too much guacamole. It has never happened.

Guacamole con piña y pepino

This fruity and crunchy "guaca" variation goes perfectly together with all types of barbecue.

Serves 4

1 cucumber
½ red onion
½–1 fresh habanero chili
2 tablespoons freshly squeezed lime juice
1 teaspoon salt
4 avocados
½ fresh pineapple
1 small bunch of fresh cilantro

Peel and dice the cucumber, finely chop the onion, mash the chili, and mix everything together with lime juice and salt. Dice the avocados and fold into the mixture. Dice the pineapple, chop the cilantro, and add just before serving.

Taco shop guacamole

The exception to the rule: Now it's okay to put the avocado in a blender. The purpose is not to save time, however, but to create a smooth sauce for tacos and barbecued meat, which is made even creamier with a little crème fraîche.

Serves 4

3 green or yellow tomatoes (not red ones)
4 tomatillos
3 garlic cloves
3 fresh green chilis, such as medium-hot chilis or jalapeños
1 teaspoon salt
1 small bunch of fresh cilantro
3 avocados
1 cup/8fl oz/240ml crème fraîche or sour cream

Boil the tomatoes, tomatillos, garlic, and salt without water (the tomatoes contribute the liquid) for about 15 minutes. Let cool. Mix in a blender with the cilantro and avocados until you have a smooth sauce. Add the crème fraîche or sour cream.

Guacamole con manzana

Only for the over 21 year olds, this "guaca" with apple, tequila, and pecans might sound a little weird, but it tastes great. Promise.

Serves 2

1 green apple
1 tablespoon tequila
1 tablespoon freshly squeezed lime juice
1 fresh green chili, such as medium-hot or jalapeño
1 teaspoon salt
½ white onion
1 cup/3½oz/100g pecans
2 avocados
fresh cilantro

Peel and dice the apple and mix together with the tequila and lime juice. Toast the chilis in a dry saucepan and mash together with the salt and onion, using a mortar and pestle. Toast the nuts in the same pan. Dice the avocados, stir in the cilantro, and mix everything together.

About tomatillos

Tomatillo is a sour fruit that tastes like a cross between a Cape gooseberry and a tomato. It can be found in jars in South American food stores or specialty delis, or fresh at specialty produce markets. You can replace them with the hard-to-find Cape gooseberries—but you won't get the same green color—or green tomatoes with a dash of lemon juice.

CHILIS AND SPICES

Chilis, dried and fresh, are an important part of Tex-Mex cuisine, and there are now so many varieties available that it's easy to get confused. Here is a short introduction to the most common varieties.

1 Jalapeño

These green little fatties are one of the most common chilis in supermarkets. They have a more consistent heat than ordinary chilis, so choose jalapeños when you can. The darker the green, the hotter the chili.

2 Guajillo

This fruity, mild chili is perfect for all kinds of pork or for salads.

3 Chili piquin

When you eat street food in Mexico, you often get a couple of these little mini chilis on your plate together with a wedge of lime. The idea is that you should be able to control the heat and the acidity yourself.

4 Spice mixes

Make a large batch of these spice mixes and store in the cupboard, then you're always ready if you want ribs or pulled pork or something. Here are a couple that are used often.

RENDEZ-VOUS DRY RUB

This useful spice mix, invented at the classic rib restaurant Rendez-vous in Memphis, Tennessee, is a perfect match for both pork and chicken.

½ cup/2oz/50g paprika
¼ cup/1½oz/40g garlic powder
¼ cup/1oz/25g chili powder
3 tablespoons ground black pepper
3 tablespoons salt
2 tablespoons whole celery seeds or fennel seeds
1 tablespoon crushed celery seeds or fennel seeds
4 teaspoons yellow mustard seeds
1 tablespoon dried oregano
1 tablespoon dried thyme
1 tablespoon whole coriander seeds
1 tablespoon crushed coriander seeds
1 tablespoon Knorr Aromat Seasoning

Mix together the dry rub in a bowl. Stored airtight, it will last a long time.

FUEGO SPICE MIX

If you'd like an all-round spice mix, easy on hand in the cupboard, this one is perfect. It can be used for everything grilled or fried—even vegetables—and to flavor your tortilla chips or popcorn.

3 tablespoons paprika
1 teaspoon cayenne pepper
1 teaspoon ground white pepper
1 tablespoon freshly ground black pepper
1 tablespoon garlic powder
1 tablespoon chili powder
1 tablespoon dried oregano
1 tablespoon salt

Mix the spices together and store in an airtight jar.

BARBECUE RUB

When slow-cooking meat in a barbecue smoker, strive for a "bark" coating. The bark is the hard, caramelized coating that locks in juices and adds flavor.

½ cup/3½oz/100g demerara sugar or
    other raw brown sugar
½ cup/3½oz/100g granulated sugar
⅓ cup/1¼oz/35g paprika
1½ tablespoons salt
1½ tablespoons garlic powder
1 tablespoon freshly ground black pepper
1 tablespoon ground ginger
1 tablespoon onion powder
1 teaspoon dried rosemary

Mix the sugars and spices together and store in an airtight jar.

5 Habanero

Fruity and more spicy than the other fresh chilis. Use with caution. Perfect for fruity salsas.

6 Chipotle

A dried and smoked jalapeño, which is a must if you are making chili. Boil or toast before making into a puree. It will add a deep, smoky flavor to your food. Often sold in packages together with ancho chilis.

7 Ancho

Dried chili that you boil or toast and then make into a puree—used in salsas or stews for an unbeatable depth in flavor. Often sold in packages together with chipotle.

8 Chili de arbol

A classic dried chili. To use, crumble with your fingers and sprinkle it over food that's far too bland.

9 Red/green chili

The most common chili in supermarkets, it can be yellow, green, or red and vary a lot in heat. So do taste before you put it into the stew.

10 Poblano

The poblano pepper looks like a large chili and tastes like a mix between a bell pepper and a jalapeño. If you can't get hold of fresh poblano, you can replace it with pointed peppers together with a chili for extra bite.

A few words on cheese

Mexican cheeses are frequently used in the West Coast states, but they can be more difficult to source in other parts of the country. However, the good news is you can replace them. **Queso fresco** is, for example, used for crumbling over tacos but can be replaced with a mild feta cheese.

Quesillo is a soft, stringy cheese, perfect for using on quesadillas and taquitos, that can be replaced with mozzarella. **Requesón** is a mild, spreadable fresh cheese used for enchiladas, that much resembles ricotta. And the originally Spanish, yellow **Manchego** cheese that is more easy to find across the USA is always prepared to step in whenever cheese is required.

10.

SALSA AND STUFF

To compare homemade salsa with a store-bought version is like comparing a three-course dinner in a fancy restaurant with eating spaghetti straight from the can while watching a reality show. The salsa is the hot, beating heart in Tex-Mex cooking, so take it seriously.

Salsa roja

The classic red salsa that, together with salsa verde, in some states is almost used in the same way as salt and pepper.

Serves 4

1 onion
4 tomatoes
6 garlic cloves
4 dried chilis, such as ancho or guajillo, seeded
½–¾ cup/3 ½–7fl oz/ 100–200ml chicken stock or broth
1 small bunch of fresh cilantro
salt

Cut the onion and tomatoes into quarters and boil together with the garlic and dried chilis in enough stock or broth so that they're just covered, for about 15 minutes. Let cool. Mix everything together in a blender with the cilantro, then strain through a strainer to remove the skin and seeds. Season to taste.

Salsa verde

This wonderful salsa uses tomatillos to get its green color and sweet-sour taste (see p. 18), but if you can't find it you can replace it with Cape gooseberries or green tomatoes and lemon juice.

Serves 4

6 tomatillos
1 white onion

3 garlic cloves
1–2 fresh chilis, such as jalapeños
1 small bunch of fresh cilantro
2 tablespoons corn oil
salt

Roast the tomatillos, white onion, garlic, and jalapeños in the oven on a high temperature until golden. Blend to a smooth salsa. Add the cilantro and blend for a little longer. Heat the oil in a saucepan, add the salsa, and reduce until nice and thick. Season with salt. Let cool.

Salsa cocida

A fresher, less hot, smooth everyday salsa that is quick to prepare.

Serves 4

12 (about 7oz/200g) cherry tomatoes
1 onion
6 garlic cloves
2–3 fresh red chilis, seeded
1 small bunch of fresh cilantro
salt

Preheat the oven to maximum. Cut the tomatoes and onion into quarters and roast together with the garlic and the chilis in the oven until charred. Let cool. Mix in a blender together with the cilantro. Season to taste.

Pico de gallo

"Pico de gallo" means the "beak of the rooster" and that's how a perfect pico should taste—like little chili-hot rooster pecks on the tongue.

Serves 4
12 (about 7oz/200g) cherry tomatoes
1 white onion
1 small bunch of fresh cilantro
1–2 fresh chilis
2 tablespoons freshly squeezed lime juice
1 teaspoon salt

Halve the tomatoes and remove the seeds. Chop together with the onion, cilantro, and chilis, the finer the better. If you don't like cilantro, use it anyway. It's time you give up such silliness. Squeeze the lime over the top and season with salt. The flavor combination of lime and salt is the linchpin of Mexican cuisine, and it's crucial you get it right. It should be acidic enough to get your mouth watering but also salty enough to balance this.

Mango salsa

This sweet-spicy, fruity salsa goes well with fish, shellfish, and pork—and is perfect for carnitas. Habanero is especially hot, so be careful, particularly if all of a sudden you have to heed nature's call...

Serves 4
2 mangoes
½ red onion
1 small bunch of fresh cilantro
1–2 tablespoons freshly squeezed lime juice
½–1 fresh habanero chili
½ teaspoon salt

Finely chop the ingredients and mix together in a bowl. Serve cold.

Salsa para mariscos

This traditional green salsa is perfect for shellfish and fish. Fresh.

Serves 4
1 cucumber
4 large ripe tomatoes
1 white onion
2 fresh chilis, such as medium-hot chilis or jalapeños
fresh cilantro, to taste
2 teaspoons salt

Peel and seed the cucumber. Finely chop the cucumber and tomatoes and put into a bowl. Then finely chop the onion, chilis, and cilantro and add to the cucumber. Add the salt and stir together a little.

Green herb salsa

Wonderfully green and fruity from the olive oil. Not a salsa for dipping but perfect for ceviche.

Serves 4
2 garlic cloves, skin left on
1–2 fresh green chilis, such as medium-hot chilis or jalapeños
2 tablespoons olive oil
1 large bunch of fresh cilantro
1 bunch of fresh parsley
1 cucumber
2 avocados
salt

Toast the garlic and chilis in a dry skillet. When they've turned a nice color, peel the garlic, seed the chilis, and mix together with the oil and the herbs in a blender. Peel and seed the cucumber and dice. Do the same for the avocado. Season to taste.

PICKLES

Pickled vegetables can be something like a crispy ketchup—with only a few easy vegetables or other simple ingredients you immediately increase the acidity, sweetness, and crunch in a dish. All of the following recipes (except perhaps the eggs) go well together with tacos and barbecue.

Pickled red onion

Pickled red onion is a Mex classic that works with pretty much all types of tacos and grilled meat. Add some liquid from a jar of pickled beets if you want to intensify the red color.

Serves 4
2 red onions
1 cup/8fl oz/240ml white wine vinegar
¼ cup/2oz/50g granulated sugar
1 tablespoon salt
1 bay leaf
½–1 fresh chili, such as habanero
1 tablespoon liquid from pickled beets (optional)

Thinly slice the onions. Mix all the other ingredients together in a saucepan and bring to a boil. Add the onions and simmer for 30 seconds. Let cool, then transfer to a screw-top jar along with the chili and seal. Refrigerate for 6–8 hours, until the onion slowly changes color from red-white to a beautiful light pink. It will keep for a couple of days in the refrigerator.

Quick pickled carrots

If you can't find the time or energy to start pickling several days in advance, you can try this quick version of pickled carrots.

1 jar
2 carrots

2 garlic cloves
1–2 fresh red or green chilis, such as medium-hot chilis or jalapeños
½ cup/4fl oz/120ml white wine vinegar
1 teaspoon salt
1 teaspoon granulated sugar
1 bay leaf
5 whole white peppercorns

Julienne the carrots evenly into long, thin strips, like matches. Slice the garlic and chilis (keep the seeds) and mix all the ingredients together for the pickling juice with ½ cup/4fl oz/120ml water. Put everything into a bowl and place in the refrigerator for 1–2 hours.

Pickled watermelon rind

Take the opportunity to make use of the rind when making agua fresca (see p. 136) and make this super sour and wonderful crunchy pickle that goes well with most things. They're also perfect as a snack on their own or together with a beer in front of the TV, or by the water somewhere.

Serves 2–4
½ watermelon
⅞ cup/7fl oz/200ml distilled white vinegar
⅞ cup/7oz/200g granulated sugar
1 tablespoon salt
1 whole star anise
1 thumb-size piece of fresh ginger

Peel the green skin from the melon and retain ¾ inch/2cm of the pink fruit flesh. You'll now have a watermelon rind made up of about half yellow-green and half pink. Cut the melon into 1¼–1½-inch/3–4-cm pieces. Put the rest of the ingredients in a pan with 1 cup/8fl oz/240ml of water and bring to a boil. Add the watermelon and simmer for 1 minute. Let cool, put into a screw-top jar, and refrigerate. It's ready to eat after 1 hour and lasts for a week.

Pickled chili

If you want to put an end to those creepy green-gray, mushy chilis from a jar, it's easy to make your own.

1 jar
12oz/350g fresh red or green chilis, such as jalapeño or medium-hot chilis
⅞ cup/7fl oz/200ml apple cider vinegar
2 tablespoons pink peppercorns
2 dried bay leaves
2 garlic cloves
2 tablespoons salt
2 tablespoons granulated sugar
1 cup/7fl oz/200ml water

Slice the chilis into rings, seeds and all, and put them into a screw-top jar. Bring the rest of the ingredients to a boil in a saucepan and simmer for 5 minutes. Pour the hot liquid over the chilis and let stand for a couple of hours before putting the jar into the refrigerator. The pickle will last for a couple of months.

Escabeche

Often served with food in Mexico, escabeche is pieces of pickled superspicy vegetables.

1 large jar
12oz/350g vegetables, such as carrots, radishes, and cauliflower (mixed together or separate)
1 red onion
1⅛ cups/9fl oz/250ml apple cider vinegar
2 tablespoons pink peppercorns
2 dried bay leaves
3 garlic cloves
2 tablespoons salt
2 tablespoons granulated sugar
1 cup/9fl oz/250ml water

Peel and cut the vegetables into small bite-size pieces. Slice the onion. Bring the rest of the ingredients to a boil in a saucepan, add the vegetables, remove from the heat, and let stand on the warm stove for 30 minutes. Let cool, put into a screw-top jar, and refrigerate for one day before you eat it. It will last for a week.

Pickled eggs

Pickled eggs are a classic snack in dive bars in the South. For those who don't really have the guts to try them, but would like to, here is the recipe.

Makes 8 snacks
8 eggs
⅔ cup/5fl oz/150ml white wine vinegar
⅔ cup/5fl oz/150ml granulated sugar
⅔ cup/5fl oz/150ml pickled beet liquid
1 tablespoon salt
⅔ cup/5fl oz/150ml water

Hard-boil the eggs and let cool. Meanwhile, bring the rest of the ingredients to a boil in a saucepan then let cool. Peel the eggs, put them into a screw-top jar and pour the pickling juice over them. Let stand overnight and the eggs will turn into a beautiful shocking pink. They will last for a couple of days in the refrigerator.

HOW TO MAKE A BARBECUE SMOKER

To quick-grill a piece of pork that's been soaking in a prepared marinade for 30 minutes is always nice—at least once a year. Although for the serious barbecue master, there's a whole world of indirect grilling to discover.

When cooking food for a barbecue, there are two routes: you either go down the more familiar route and grill your hot dogs and burgers, meat, fish, or vegetables using direct heat, where you place whatever you want cooked on the grill rack directly over the coals until it's done. It's quick, easy, and tasty—but not always. Because sometimes you might want a more intense barbecue kick, and that's when it's time to start experimenting with indirect heat when you want to have a barbecue.

Barbecue in a kettle grill?

Does smoke-cooking meat in a kettle grill work? Yes, actually. It's what that little separator you've probably put away in the garage somewhere is for. Just place it in the middle of the grill, put the coal on one side and a can of water on the other, and then follow the same instructions as for the barbecue smoker.

Indeed, the world's best barbecues are found in Texas, where in the nineteenth century a unique barbecue culture emerged that is still alive and kicking today. As with so many things in America, it's a result of how different groups of people have met and become inspired by each other. Beautiful. German immigrants used to smoke sausages and meat in their home country and brought their food habits to the new country. Gradually the cowboys' "fire pits" (holes in the ground that food was cooked in on the prairie) as well as the Mexicans' traditional "barbacoa" were incorporated in the same style.

The result was a cooking method somewhere in between smoking and charcoal grilling and with flavors that at one and the same time reminds you of German polka, country twang, and the Mexicans' giant guitars. Delicious.

This kind of barbecue basically means that you cook the meat using indirect heat, with plenty of wood chips for creating plenty of yummy smoke in a grill often made out of an oil drum. Firewood is also okay to use, of course. The meat is placed in one half of the grill, the charcoal and the wood chips in the other, with a lid down on top so that the heat and smoke don't escape. The result is an extremely smoky and tender piece of meat that tastes as if a piece of heaven just fell down on your plate.

This method might take a little longer than cooking over a direct heat, but it's neither especially difficult nor a lot of effort to cook this way. You just have to work out the right temperature in the grill, put the meat on the rack, and sit down with a beer or listen to the weather forecast or something. The benefits to gain from this cooking method are also many: in addition to the smoky flavor, the low heat and long cooking time—low and slow are the catchwords—break down the meat fibers so that the more flavorful, but tougher details become tender and amazingly tasty. Contrary to what you might think, smoke-grilled slow-cooked meat will also be juicier than the quickly prepared piece of meat, when far too much water evaporates.

This means that you need to keep checking the temperature when cooking with indirect heat; a normal oven thermometer that you buy for ten bucks in your local homeware store is the indirect barbecue master's best friend. Control the heat with the amount of charcoal you add, and if it gets too hot, you just have to lift the lid a little (think of an oven). If you don't want to go too fancy with a superexpensive, commercial smoker barbecue (that will last for only three seasons anyway), it's easy and cheap to make your own.

What you need

Most barbecue masters in Texas agree, the best smoker grills are the ones you make yourself. Budget about $50–75 for the materials.

Tools
angle grinder
drill
pencil
angle ruler
ruler
carpenter's level
a good mood

Materials
1 unused oil drum (you run the risk of poisoning yourself if you go with a used one)
1 handle
2 hinges
at least 1½-inch/4-cm long bolts and nuts in suitable widths
4 brackets
1 supporting frame of some kind
1 grill rack

What to do

1 Measure the quarter, or wedge, of the drum that is to be cut out and used as a lid. Look at the picture on p. 32. Make sure that the drum's bolt holes (all drums have these) are positioned down in the grill so that the fire will get some oxygen.
2 Use an angle grinder to cut out your measured wedge.
3 Work out where to put the holes for the hinges and the handle for the lid. Drill and bolt together. Do the same with the brackets that will support the grill rack.
4 Cut the supporting frame so that the drum can lie down securely. Exactly how to do this depends on what kind of supporting frame you've found. Search in a scrapyard.
5 The grill rack you can either buy second-hand from a scrapyard or new in a store that sells barbecue accessories. Choose a rack made out of cast iron for best results and remember it should not cover the whole of the grill—if it does, it will be difficult to add more charcoal during cooking.
6 This simple smoker can also be used as a normal grill. Just place the coals directly under the meat and grill as usual.

PART 2

BREAKFAST

The most important meal of the day doesn't have to be the most boring. A couple of pancakes with maple syrup and ice cream, or a breakfast taco with a salsa so hot that it grabs you by the collar and cuffs you into shape is, in my opinion, the perfect way to start the day.

CHILAQUILES

Chilaquiles are the ultimate hangover breakfast. And it's easy to understand why: it's crispy, eggy, and hot.

SERVES 1

2 corn tortillas (see p. 12)
2 eggs
salt
a dash of milk
oil, for frying
2–4 tablespoons salsa verde (see p. 25)
feta cheese
1 handful of chopped fresh cilantro
½ red onion
1 fresh green chili, such as jalapeño
radishes

Either put the corn tortillas in the oven until crispy or deep-fry to nachos. With a fork, whisk together the eggs, salt, and milk.

Add the tortilla chips and mix. Sauté the mixture slowly in an oiled skillet, stirring constantly so that the eggs cover the tortilla chips and everything turns nice and creamy.

Drizzle the salsa over the egg mixture, crumble the feta over the top, add cilantro, onion, chili, and thinly sliced radishes, and devour.

Chilaquiles rojos

If mixing tortilla chips in eggs feels somewhat weird, you can always do it the other way around— first mix them with salsa, then fry the egg and place on top. There are many variations of this much-loved dish.

Serves 1
2 corn tortillas (see p. 12)
2–3 tablespoons salsa roja (see p. 25)
1 egg
feta cheese

Preheat the oven to 400°F/200°C. Cover the tortilla chips in salsa and bake in the oven for 10 minutes. Fry the egg and place on top. Crumble the feta over the top.

HUEVOS RANCHEROS

"The ranch owner's eggs" is the name of this incredibly easy, but also incredibly tasty, breakfast. Don't be afraid of the poaching. Just remember to use fresh eggs.

SERVES 4

1 tablespoon white wine vinegar
4 fresh eggs
4 corn or wheat tortillas (see p. 12)
1 quantity of salsa roja or salsa cocida (see p. 25)
feta cheese

Bring a saucepan of water to a boil, add a dash of vinegar, and stir the water vigorously with a wooden spoon so that you create a small swirl.

Crack the egg into a small cup and drop it quickly into the water, cover with a lid, remove the pan from the heat, and let the egg stand for 3 minutes before taking it out, using a slotted spoon or skimmer.

Warm up a corn tortilla, add a spoonful of salsa, and top with the poached egg. Grate feta cheese on top like a boss.

Huevos divorciados

Literally means divorced eggs—but instead of infidelity, it's one green and one red salsa that keep them apart in this instance. Clever.

Serves 1
2 eggs
1 corn tortilla
1–2 tablespoons salsa verde (see p. 25)
1–2 tablespoons salsa roja (see p. 25)

Fry the eggs and place them on top of the tortilla. Dollop one kind of salsa over each egg.

PANCAKES

There are endless variations on pancakes, making it difficult to choose a favorite, but I can tell you that these three are the absolute most scrumptious ones: banana pancakes; coconut and lime pancakes; and finally, cinnamon and apple pancakes.

SERVES 4

2 cups/9oz/250g all-purpose flour
2 teaspoons baking powder
1/2 teaspoon salt
1 tablespoon granulated sugar
1 cup/8fl oz/240ml milk
2 tablespoons melted butter, plus
    butter for frying
1 egg

COCONUT AND LIME PANCAKE
3 1/2 cups/9oz/250g dry unsweetened
    coconut, toasted
finely grated zest and juice of 1 lime
1 teaspoon ground cinnamon

BANANA PANCAKE
2–3 bananas

CINNAMON AND APPLE PANCAKE
2 apples
2 tablespoons butter
2 tablespoons packed light
    brown sugar
1 tablespoon ground cinnamon

Mix the dry ingredients for the batter together. Add the milk and whisk, followed by the melted butter and finally the egg.

If you want to make coconut and lime pancakes, add the coconut, lime, and cinnamon straight to the batter.

If you want to make banana pancakes, slice the bananas and press them down on the pancake just after you've put the batter into the skillet.

And if you want to make cinnamon apples, slice the apples and sauté them over medium heat together with the butter, sugar, and cinnamon for about 10 minutes or until soft. Place the fried apples on top of the finished pancakes like a turbo-fueled preserve.

As for the pancakes, cook the batter in a pat of butter in a skillet. Make them either a normal size (about 4 inches/10cm) or as silver dollars (mini versions). When you see bubbles appearing on the top, it's time to flip them over.

Serve with maple syrup and vanilla ice cream, store-bought or homemade (see p. 116).

BREAKFAST TACO

Tacos for breakfast? Is that really possible? Yes, it's not only possible, it's even encouraged, especially when they're as good as this one.

SERVES 1

1 small piece uncooked chorizo
1 potato
oil, for frying
2 eggs
1 teaspoon milk
salt
1 pat of butter
1–2 tablespoons salsa roja (see p. 25)
2–4 small corn tortillas (see p. 12)

Tip!

The taco is easily transformed into a breakfast burrito if you swap the sausage for bacon and the corn tortilla for wheat. Drizzle with the salsa.

Remove the skin from the uncooked chorizo, then crumble into small pieces and cook in a skillet until nice and crispy. You don't need frying oil. The chorizo is fatty enough.

Peel and julienne the potato and deep-fry in hot oil until golden and crispy. Drain on paper towels.

Make scrambled eggs by whisking together the eggs with a dash of milk and some salt, and cook superslowly in butter over low heat while stirring constantly until nice and creamy.

Build the breakfast taco by first spreading the tortilla with salsa, then add a dollop of scrambled eggs, followed by sausage and topped with a pile of potatoes. Delicious.

PART 3

ANTOJITOS

The word "antojitos" means that feeling you have when you're a bit hungry and want a small bite of something—and hungry is just what you will feel when getting introduced to these Tex-Mex snacks. Everything from enchiladas via nachos to tostados.

TRUCK STOP ENCHILADA

These are a variation on fast-food chain tacos, which are a watered-down version of Mexican cuisine. But in neither genuine Tex-Mex nor Mexican versions is ground beef used—it's a lazy shortcut to achieve that stringy, melt-in-the-mouth consistency of the slow-cooked meat used in a genuine chili.

SERVES 6

12 large wheat tortillas (see p. 12)
1 quantity of salsa roja (see p. 25)
1 quantity of beef chili (see p. 70)
1³/₄ cups/7oz/200g grated cheddar or
   Manchego cheese
1³/₄ cups/7oz/200g grated mozzarella

Preheat the oven to 400°F/ 200°C. Dip the tortillas in the salsa—enchiladas literally means "dipped in chili"—add a dollop of beef chili, and most of the cheese.

Roll together and place in an ovenproof dish. Drizzle with the remaining salsa, sprinkle with the rest of the cheese, and bake in the oven for 10 minutes, or until it's bubbling.

Serve with chopped cilantro, white onion, and sour cream.

BAJA CEVICHE

There's nothing that tastes like summer more than tortilla chips dipped in lime-marinated raw fish. To make the snazzy ice bowls on p. 50, put ice cubes into a bowl, press a smaller bowl into the ice, fill it up with water, and then put the whole lot in the freezer.

SERVES 6

CLASSIC CEVICHE

1lb/450g firm white fish of sushi standard, such as halibut

1¼ cups/10fl oz/300ml freshly squeezed lime juice

1 white onion

2 fresh chilis, such as medium-hot chilis or jalapeños

½ cup/3½oz/100g green olives

1 large tomato

1 large bunch of fresh cilantro

2 tablespoons olive oil

salt

GREEN CUCUMBER CEVICHE

1lb/450g firm white fish of sushi standard, such as halibut

1 quantity of green herb salsa (see p. 26)

½ cup/4fl oz/120ml freshly squeezed lime juice

CLASSIC CEVICHE

Cut the fish into cubes and "cook" by marinating in the lime juice for 30–60 minutes in the refrigerator. If you're on the cautious side, you can leave them for up to 3 hours, but the fish will be cooked all the way through (that's what lime does to it). Use a nonreactive stainless steel bowl or glass bowl. Drain off the lime, finely chop the vegetables and cilantro, and add to the fish along with the olive oil and mix. Add salt to taste. Eat within 1 hour.

GREEN CUCUMBER CEVICHE

Cut the fish into dipping-friendly-size cubes and mix together with the salsa and the lime juice. Let marinate for at least 30 minutes, but a maximum of 1 hour.

Serve with deep-fried corn tortilla chips (see p. 13) to scoop it up with.

NACO DE NACHOS

Nachos with melted cheese we all know, right? This variation is much tastier and can, depending on how much cheese you add, be both a calorie bomb and actually healthy.

SERVES 4

9oz/250g flank or tenderloin steak
salt and freshly ground black pepper
oil, for frying
4 small corn tortillas (see p. 12)
grated cheese, either feta or cheddar

SOY MARINADE
1 cup/8fl oz/240ml pineapple juice
freshly squeezed juice of 1 lime
$\frac{1}{2}$ cup/4fl oz/120ml Japanese soy sauce
1 teaspoon chopped garlic
1 teaspoon ground cumin
salt and freshly ground black pepper

REFRIED BEANS
1 dried chipotle chili
3 garlic cloves
$\frac{1}{2}$ brown onion
3oz/85g bacon slices
corn oil, for frying
2 teaspoons ground cumin
1 teaspoon dried oregano
1 (15-oz/425-g) can black beans, drained
salt and freshly ground black pepper

Serve with chunky guacamole (see p. 17), chopped cilantro, and white onion or your choice of pickles.

Combine the ingredients for the marinade, add the steak, and marinate for at least 1 hour. Grill quickly on a barbecue grill or using a ridged grill pan. Season with salt and pepper.

To make the refried beans, remove the stem and seeds from the dried chili, cover with $\frac{1}{3}$–1 cup/3–8fl oz/ 90–240ml of water and boil for about 15 minutes. Meanwhile, chop and sauté the garlic and onion together with the bacon in a little oil. Season with the cumin and oregano and add the can of drained black beans. Mix the chipotle and the water together in a blender, add to the bean mixture, and let cook over low heat for about 15 minutes. Add a little more water, if needed. Add salt and pepper to taste. Mash about a third of the beans with a fork and stir.

Preheat the oven to maximum. Now you have two options: Either place the tortillas on a baking pan and spread the beans on top. Cut the grilled meat into fine strips and place on top. Add feta if you want to take it easy, cheddar if you want to crank it up. Place in the oven for 6 minutes, or until the cheese has melted and the tortilla looks crunchy. Take out and cut into 4 pieces.

Or divide the tortilla into 4 pieces, deep-fry them, and place the bean mixture, meat, and the cheese on top and chuck it in the oven.

TORTILLA SOUP

The problem with soup is that it's rarely crispy. This ingenious soup, however, is comfortingly hot and satisfyingly crunchy at the same time.

SERVES 4-6

1 (3-lb/1.3kg) whole chicken
5 tomatoes
5 brown onions
5-6 fresh red or green chilis, such as medium-hot chilis or jalapeños
3 garlic cloves
1 large bunch of fresh cilantro
2 carrots
3 celery stalks
3 potatoes
8 small corn tortillas (see p. 12)
oil, for deep-frying
4 avocados
1 lime
1 white onion
salt

Tips!

The corn tortilla cannot be replaced with wheat tortilla, but, in a worst case scenario, they can be replaced with store-bought tortilla chips.

Halve the chicken and boil in 8½ cups/3½ pints/2 liters water for about 1 hour.

Preheat the oven to 440°F/225°C. Cut the tomatoes, 1 brown onion, 2 chilis, and the garlic into large chunks. Place in a baking pan and bake in the oven for about 10 minutes. Once they are starting to brown, put everything in a blender together with half of the cilantro. Remove the chicken from the water and remove any debris and fat floating around on the surface.

Dice the carrots, the remaining brown onions, the celery, and potatoes. Add the root vegetables and the tomato sauce to the chicken stock and bring to a boil. Reduce the heat and simmer for about 25 minutes. Meanwhile, cut the corn tortillas into fine strips and deep-fry until golden and crispy. Dice the avocado and put into a bowl, then slice the remaining chilis and put into another one. Cut the lime into wedges and put into a bowl and chop the white onion and the remaining cilantro, and—that's right—put into a bowl.

Pick the meat off the chicken, discarding the skin, then tear the meat into smaller pieces and put into a bowl. Serve by letting your guests fill their soup bowl with meat and the other trimmings. Season the soup with salt and ladle over the chicken. Garnish with a handful of the deep-fried tortilla chips.

SHRIMP TAQUITOS

Shrimp taquitos are small crispy corn tortilla wraps that are the perfect finger food and extremely dip friendly. Just make sure you use thin corn tortillas, preferably purchased from a Latin American store or specialty deli, or else they can break.

SERVES 6

½ white onion
2 garlic cloves
1-2 fresh red or green chilis, such as medium-hot chilis
1 tablespoon olive oil
2 tomatoes
7-11oz/200-300g fresh peeled shrimp
1 small bunch of fresh cilantro
oil, for deep-frying
12 thin small corn tortillas (see p. 12)
1¾ cups/7oz/200g grated mozzarella
salt

Finely chop and sauté the onion, garlic, and chilis in the oil until soft. Blanch the tomatoes and remove the skin as well as the seeds. Chop and cook together with the onion mix until you get a consistency similar to ketchup.

Chop the shrimp and add to the mixture. Finely chop the cilantro and add to the mixture.

Heat the oil for deep-frying to about 365°F/185°C Dip the corn tortilla into the oil for about 1 second to soften. Spread about 3 tablespoons of the shrimp mixture on each tortilla, sprinkle with the mozzarella, roll up into a cylindrical wrap, and skewer in pairs on a soaked bamboo skewer so that you've got something to hold onto.

Deep-fry for about 2 minutes, until crispy, then season with salt. Get dipping.

Serve with salsa of your choice (see p. 25) and perhaps a guacamole (see p. 17).

ENCHILADAS SUIZAS

Despite the name, these are not Swiss enchiladas, they're just called this because of the crème fraîche-based sauce. If you can't find fresh tomatillos, you can use canned ones or even a mixture of unripe green tomatoes and Cape gooseberries. The important thing is to get the acidity right.

SERVES 4

1¼ cups/10fl oz/300ml chicken stock
    or broth
1 cup/8fl oz/240ml crème fraîche or
    sour cream
1 quantity of salsa verde (see p. 25)
salt and freshly ground black pepper
2 potatoes
2 carrots
1 rutabaga
3 tablespoons olive oil,
    plus extra for drizzling
14oz/400g uncooked chorizo
6 large or 12 small wheat tortillas
    (see p. 12)
1 cup/4oz/120g grated Manchego or
    cheddar cheese
1 cup/4oz/120g grated mozzarella

Preheat the oven to 400°F/200°C. Add the chicken stock or broth and crème fraîche or sour cream to the salsa verde, then season with salt and pepper.

Dice the root vegetables into ½-inch/1-cm cubes, drizzle with olive oil, sprinkle with salt, and roast in the oven for about 20 minutes, until crispy.

Remove the skin from the uncooked chorizo and crumble the meat into a hot saucepan with the 3 tablespoons olive oil and sauté until cooked.

To assemble the enchilada, dip the tortilla in the salsa, put the sausage and root vegetables on top, roll into a wrap, and place side by side in an ovenproof dish. Alternatively, if you use small tortillas, stack into a pile instead, like a round lasagne (see picture). This is called a stacked enchilada and is a method often used in New Mexico. Drizzle with the rest of the salsa, add the grated cheeses, and bake for about 10 minutes or until the cheese is golden.

Serve with chopped white onion, crème fraîche, and fresh cilantro.

Tres tostadas

RECIPES P. 66

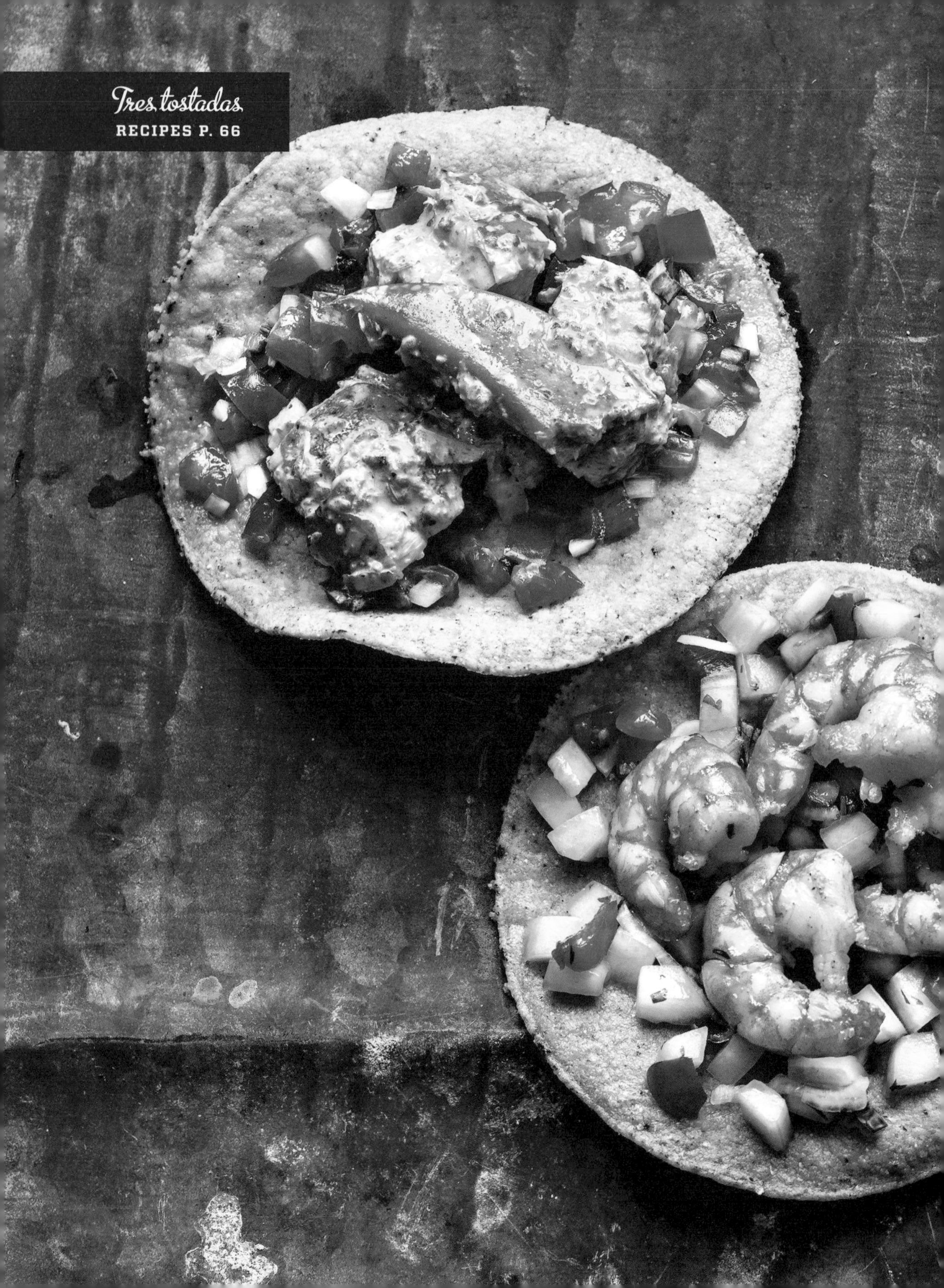

TRES TOSTADAS

A tostada is simply a deep-fried corn tortilla with plenty of lovely goodies on top—much like a crispy taco. Eat it like a Mexican crisp bread.

Creamy lobster tostada

Lobster, mayonnaise, chili—you get the idea.

Makes 4 tostadas

1 fresh poblano chili (or 1 pointed pepper and 1 standard fresh chili)
4 garlic cloves
3 tablespoons mayonnaise
salt
1 whole boiled lobster
4 corn tortillas (see p. 12)
oil, for deep-frying
½ quantity of pico de gallo (see p. 26)

Roast the poblano chili/pointed pepper together with the garlic (keep the skin on). They're ready when the skin is black. Peel and blend together with the mayonnaise. Season with salt to taste and stir in the lobster meat. Deep-fry a whole corn tortilla and drain on paper towels. Top with a spoonful of salsa and some lobster mixture and eat.

Devil shrimp tostada

These hot and buttery shrimp also make a tasty taco-filler (like everything else).

Makes 4 tostadas

salt and freshly ground black pepper
1–2 teaspoons chili powder
5 garlic cloves
2–3 tablespoons butter
7–11oz/200–300g peeled fresh shrimp
1 lime
4 corn tortillas (see p. 12)
oil, for deep-frying

½ quantity of salsa para mariscos (see p. 26)

Mash together the salt, pepper, chili powder, and garlic, using a mortar and pestle. Melt the butter in a skillet and sauté the garlic mixture. Add the peeled shrimp and warm through for up to 1 minute—not too long, or they will become dry. Squeeze lime on top. Deep-fry a whole corn tortilla, then drain on paper towels. Top with a spoonful of salsa and some shrimp and eat.

Green scallop tostada

Ceviche-style tostada

Makes 4 tostadas

3–4 limes
3 fresh chilis, such as jalapeños
salt
11oz/300g fresh scallops
½ cucumber
1 bunch of radishes
4 corn tortillas (see p. 12)
oil, for deep-frying

Squeeze the lime and mix with the chilis until a green juice appears. Strain to get rid of the pieces and season with salt. Thinly slice the scallops and let marinate in the lime juice for up to 1 hour. Peel the cucumber, remove the seeds, and slice thinly. Slice the radishes too. Deep-fry a whole corn tortilla and drain on paper towels. Top with the stuff.

Right: Pickled watermelon rind (p. 30)

Tips!

Make pickled watermelon rind (see p. 30) to go with your tostadas. Don't forget the beer.

PART 4

TACOS

A taco served with an ice-cold beer must be the best street food in the world. So scrumptious, so portable, and so rich in variation; almost anything can be stuffed in between a couple of tortilla rounds, and almost anything is. Turn the page to find out how to make the world's best taco at home.

BEEF CHILI TACO

Frank X. Tolbert was a chili lover who dedicated his life to finding the perfect chili recipe. This is what he discovered: No tomato, no beans, and just a whole lot of chili. This chili is hot, of course, but it's a kind of muffled, rumbling heat, almost like a caress.

SERVES 4

1 dried chipotle chili
1-2 dried chilis, such ancho
about 2¼lb/1kg braising steak,
   such as chuck shoulder or blade
1 whole garlic bulb
corn oil, for frying
2-3 tablespoons all-purpose flour
1 tablespoon chili powder
2 teaspoons dried oregano
2 teaspoons ground cumin
2 teaspoons dried coriander
1 tablespoon granulated sugar
salt and freshly ground black pepper
1-2 fresh chilis
1½ cups/12fl oz/350ml beer
1 beef bouillon cube

Remove the stems and seeds from the dried chilis. Cover with ½–1 cup/120–240ml water and boil for about 15 minutes. Dice the steak and finely chop the garlic, then cook the meat and garlic in a little oil. Cook in small small batches to get a nice searing of the meat.

Dust the fried meat with flour, chili powder, the other dried herbs and spices, the sugar, and salt and pepper. Finely chop and add the fresh chilis. Process the boiled chilis and water together in a blender or food processor and pour over the stew. Add the beer and bouillon cube so that it just covers the meat.

Cover with a lid and let simmer for at least 2 hours, or until the meat is tender and thready.

Serve with small wheat or corn tortillas (see p. 12), wedges of lime, sour cream or crème fraîche, chopped cilantro, white onion, and grated cheddar cheese.

GREEN SCALLOP TACO

There's something satisfying about matching the color of different foods, right? This super easy salsa (also great on your breakfast eggs) has a beautiful Green Hulk color, so choose a fresh green chili that won't ruin that effect.

SERVES 4

16 fresh scallops
salt and freshly ground black pepper
peanut oil, for frying
butter, for frying
1 quantity of green herb salsa
   (see p. 26)
lime juice, to taste

Tip!

If you don't want to sauté the scallops, do a ceviche instead—just marinate in lime juice for 10 minutes.

Pat the scallops with some paper towels until completely dry (if they're wet, they won't turn a nice color). Season with salt and pepper. Heat a saucepan with some peanut oil until really hot, then add the scallops. Now for the tricky part: You must absolutely not move the scallops about, and at the same time, of course, you'd like a nice caramelized crust that isn't burned—so how do you do it? Well, wait a couple of minutes and when your intuition says they're starting to get done, lift one of them carefully and take a peak underneath. If it looks the same as in a restaurant, you flip them over, add a dollop of butter, and let sear on the other side as well—at the same time as you spoon over the melted butter from the pan. Tasty!

Remember that a thoroughly cooked scallop is not an alternative so if you don't like half-cooked seafood, do another recipe instead.

When they're done, place 2 scallops on each tortilla, spoon the salsa over them, squeeze with lime juice to taste, and enjoy.

Serve with small wheat or corn tortillas (see p. 12) and lime wedges.

TACO AL PASTOR

Taco al pastor is roughly the Mexican equivalent of shawarma, where marinated meat is placed on a rotating vertical spit and grilled for hours. Yum! It's much easier to make al pastor at home.

SERVES 4

1 teaspoon cumin seeds
1/2 teaspoon dried oregano
2 large garlic cloves
1/2 white onion
2 dried chilis, such as ancho
5–10 other dried chilis, depending on strength and taste
2 tablespoons apple cider vinegar
2 teaspoons salt
2 tablespoons freshly squeezed lime juice
1 pineapple, with top and bottom removed, peeled, and cored
2¼lb/1kg boneless pork shoulder

Preheat the oven to maximum. Toast the cumin seeds in a dry saucepan and crush together with the oregano in a mortar and pestle (or use ground cumin if you must). Set aside. Put the garlic and onion on a baking sheet without oil and put into the oven until they've begun to brown.

Halve the dried chilis, remove the stems and seeds, and boil in 1/2–1 cup/ 4–8fl oz/120–240ml water for about 15 minutes. Blend everything together and add the crushed spices, vinegar, salt, lime juice, half of the pineapple (reserve the other half until later), the roasted onion and garlic, and blend. Let cool.

Slice the pork, drizzle with half of the marinade (reserve the other half in the refrigerator), and let marinate for 4 hours or overnight.

When it's time to eat, slice the reserved half of the pineapple and grill on a hot ridged grill pan or barbecue grill. Take the meat out of the marinade and let it drain a little, then grill quickly over high heat. Slice the meat thinly and serve with the reserved marinade slightly heated up—be careful to not mix it up with the marinade used for marinating the meat or you might end up with a stomach ache.

Serve with small wheat or corn tortillas (see p. 12), or salsa verde or salsa roja (see p. 25), as well as chopped white onion.

BAJA FISH TACO

Fish and coleslaw might not sound particularly appetizing, but I promise you—baja fish taco is the king of tacos.

SERVES 4

¾ cup/3½oz/100g all-purpose flour

2 teaspoons chili powder

2 teaspoons ground cumin

1 tablespoon paprika

salt

1 egg

1 cup/3½oz/100g panko bread crumbs (or more if needed)

oil, for deep-frying

1¼lb/600g fish fillets, such as tuna steak, sea bass, or halibut

COLESLAW

1 tablespoon freshly squeezed lime juice

1 tablespoon Dijon mustard

2 garlic cloves, crushed

2 egg yolks

1 cup/8fl oz/240ml corn oil

lime zest, to taste

salt and freshly ground black pepper

¼ red or green cabbage

Mix the lime juice, mustard, garlic, and egg yolks together for the coleslaw. Pour the oil into the mix slowly while whisking with an electric mixer. Be careful so it doesn't split. Add lime zest and salt and pepper to taste.

Finely shred the cabbage and mix with the garlic mayonnaise—don't use too much, just enough so the cabbage is covered. Put it into the refrigerator.

Just before it's time to eat, mix the flour and the spices together on a plate, whisk the egg and put onto another plate, and put the panko onto a third. Heat an inch or two of oil in a deep skillet or a saucepan. First dip the fish fillets into the spiced flour, followed by the egg, and finally into the panko. Drop into the hot oil. Deep-fry for a couple of minutes on each side, until the panko bread crumbs have turned brown, then drain on paper towels.

Serve with small wheat or corn tortillas (see p. 12), mango salsa (see p. 26), and crumbled feta cheese.

CARNITA TACO

The definition of "carnitas" is "little meats," and that's just what this is—small pieces of pork boiled in Coca-Cola and spices until transformed into a thready, chewy, and sweet-spicy goo that you will love for the rest of your life.

SERVES 4

2¼lb/1kg boneless pork shoulder
2 tablespoons fuego spice mix
   (see p. 21)
1 lime
1 orange
1 tablespoon Chinese soy sauce
1 tablespoon ground cumin
5 garlic cloves
2¼ cups/18fl oz/500ml Coca-Cola
   (not diet)

Cut the pork into small cubes and massage the fuego spice mix into the meat. Squeeze lime and orange over the meat, then add the soy and cumin. Finely chop and add the garlic and let marinate for at least 1 hour, but preferably overnight.

Take the meat out of the marinade, save the marinade, and sauté the meat. Once the meat has browned, you can add the marinade. Open the Coca-Cola and pour in until the meat is covered. Top up when needed. Cover with a lid and let simmer for at least 2 hours.

Remove the lid toward the end and let cook until you've got a wonderful, sticky goo.

Serve with small wheat or corn tortillas (see p. 12), guacamole of your choice (see p. 17), and mango salsa (see p. 26).

CRISPY SHRIMP TACO

Fried jumbo shrimp are delicious. But make sure they're wild caught. Anything else is just evil. If you can't find any, use regular cooked shrimp or firm white fish cut into shrimp-sized pieces. Don't forget the quick pickled carrots to go with it.

SERVES 4

¾ cup/3½oz/100g all-purpose flour
1 teaspoon salt
1 egg
1 tablespoon milk
2⅓ cups/7oz/200g panko bread crumbs
oil, for deep-frying
7–11oz/200–300g peeled fresh shrimp

CHILI MAYO
1 tablespoon Dijon mustard
1 tablespoon freshly squeezed
   lime juice
2 garlic cloves, crushed
2 egg yolks
1 cup/8fl oz/240ml corn oil
salt and freshly ground black pepper
1–2 tablespoons pickled chili
   (see p. 31)

Make a mayonnaise by mixing together the mustard, lime juice, garlic, and egg yolks. Pour the oil into the mixture slowly while whisking with an electric mixer. Be careful so it doesn't split. Add salt and pepper to taste. Blend home-pickled chili until smooth and stir into the mayonnaise. Take a second to feel proud of your homemade mayo before getting started on the pickled carrots.

When you're ready to eat, just mix the flour and salt on a plate, whisk the egg and put on another plate, and put the panko bread crumbs onto a third. Heat an inch or two of oil in a deep skillet or a saucepan. First dip the shrimp into the spiced flour, followed by the egg, and finally into the panko bread crumbs. To jazz it up a little, you can leave the tails unpeeled. Drop into the hot oil and deep-fry for about 1 minute on each side, until the panko bread crumbs have turned a nice brown, then drain on paper towels.

Serve with small wheat or corn tortillas (see p. 12), thinly sliced avocados, white onion, and some lime wedges.

BEER-BRAISED LAMB SHANK TACO

Everyone likes dipping, right? There are few things that are nicer to dip in than the leftover juices from beer-braised lamb shank. So pour it into a bowl and serve on the side.

SERVES 4

3 tablespoons chili powder

2 tablespoons ground cumin

1 tablespoon dried coriander

1$\frac{1}{2}$ teaspoons ground cinnamon

about 3$\frac{1}{4}$lb/1.5kg medium lamb
   shanks on the bone

corn oil, for frying

2$\frac{3}{4}$ cups/1$\frac{1}{4}$ pints/660ml dark beer

$\frac{1}{4}$ cup/2fl oz/60ml apple cider vinegar

2 tablespoons tomato paste

salt and freshly ground black pepper

Mix the dry ingredients in a bowl, then pat onto the lamb shanks.

Heat some oil in a cast-iron Dutch oven or a casserole dish, then sear the shanks for 2–3 minutes on each side. Reduce the heat and add the beer, vinegar, and tomato paste. Cover with a lid and let simmer for 2–4 hours. Remove the lid toward the end of cooking and reduce the braising juices a little. Add salt and pepper to taste.

Pull the meat off the bone with a fork and serve together with the braising juices poured into a separate bowl for dipping the tacos.

Serve with small wheat or corn tortillas (see p. 12), thinly sliced avocados, white onion, and some lime wedges.

PART 5

BARBECUES

What do you get if you mix German sausage smoking with Mexican *barbacoa* and cowboy fire pits? Answer: The world's best barbecue culture. Turn the page for a mouth-watering basic course.

PULLED PORK

Pulled pork has become a barbecue classic, and all it needs is bread, coleslaw, and perhaps some crispy pork crackling as accompaniments. It's a dish worthy of a barbecue-craving king or queen. It will, of course, taste better if cooked on an outdoor barbecue grill than in the oven.

SERVES 4

about 2³/₄lb/1.2kg pork shoulder or
    Boston butt on the bone
barbecue rub (see p. 22)

*Cook on
indirect heat*

For exact method
see p. 34.

Serve with *homemade burger buns (see pp. 13–14), apple coleslaw (see p. 105), and barbecue sauce (see p. 105). Alternatively, with homemade burger buns, taco-shop guacamole (see p. 18), and pickled red onion (see p. 30).*

OUTDOOR BARBECUE:
Massage the barbecue rub into the meat, then place it on the part of the grill rack without any charcoal below. It shouldn't get too hot, 230–248°F/110–120°C. (Don't cheat.) The sugar in the rub will caramelize into a hard coating that makes the outside crispy and the inside juicy. Place a plate filled with water under the meat so that it doesn't get too dry, throw a handful of wood-smoking chips on the burning charcoal, and cover with the lid. Throw some handfuls of wood chips over the coal every 30 minutes for 2¹/₂ hours. Wrap the meat in aluminum foil and grill on an indirect heat until the meat starts to break off when you're poking it but is still juicy. Allow 2–3 hours per 2¹/₂lb/1.2kg of meat.

OVEN:
Preheat the oven to 230°F/110°C (use an oven thermometer). Massage the barbecue rub into the meat before placing it in an ovenproof dish and roasting in the oven. Roast until the inside temperature reaches 203°F/95°C, which could take up to 6 hours, then turn the oven off and let the roast cool in the oven for about 2 hours.

WHEN THE MEAT IS DONE:
Let rest, then pull it apart, using two forks. It should break easily and be thready. If you want, you can mix in more spice mix.

CARNE ASADA

Grilled meat and some guacamole—it doesn't have to be more complicated than that to throw a party. Both hanger and flank steak are chewy but rich in flavor (and cheap). The kiwi in the marinade contains an enzyme that tenderizes the meat.

SERVES 4

1 whole hanger steak or flank steak
(about 2¼lb/1kg)

MARINADE
juice of 1 lime
¼ cup/2fl oz/60ml olive oil
1 small bunch of fresh cilantro
1 fresh red or green chili, such as
medium-hot chili
½ kiwi
3 garlic cloves
1 teaspoon granulated sugar
½ teaspoon dried oregano
¼ teaspoon ground cumin
2 teaspoons salt
freshly ground black pepper

Mix all the ingredients for the marinade together in a bowl, add the meat and turn to coat, then cover and let marinate overnight in the refrigerator.

OUTDOOR BARBECUE:
Just before lighting the grill, take the meat out of the refrigerator and let rest at room temperature. When the flames have died down and the charcoals are white and hot, place the meat directly above. Throw a couple of handfuls of soaked mesquite wood chips on the coals and close the lid so your meat gets that really smoky flavor as well as the beautiful red color. Grill for a couple of minutes on each side and remove the meat while it feels juicy. Let rest for 5 minutes, then slice thinly, across the fibers of the meat.

OVEN:
Preheat the oven to 400°F/200°C. It also works to cook on a ridged grill pan on the stove, but remember the pan has to be so hot that it's smoking. Finish off by placing the meat in the oven for a couple of minutes.

Serve with small wheat or corn tortillas (see p. 12), chunky guacamole (see p. 17), crumbled feta cheese, and pickled red onion (see p. 30).

CHILI CHEESEBURGER

A really good hamburger should be crispy on the outside and so juicy inside that you have to lean over a plate to keep the juices from running down your front. The secret is not adding a secret ingredient, but the other way around—it's what you don't add. A real hamburger has only three ingredients: beef, salt, and freshly ground black pepper.

SERVES 4

1³/₄lb/800g freshly ground flank, chuck shoulder, or chuck blade steak
salt and freshly ground black pepper
2 green pointed peppers
2–3 fresh green chilis
4 slices of American cheese, cheddar cheese, or Swiss cheese
4 homemade burger buns (see pp. 13–14), halved

Go to the butcher and buy a cheap but fatty piece of beef, such as flank steak, chuck shoulder steak, or chuck blade steak, and ask them to grind it. When you're back home, mix the ground meat with salt and pepper and shape into 4 patties. Get the barbecue grill going. Char the pointed peppers and the chilis until the skins turn black, place them in a plastic bag, and after a couple of minutes, peel the skins off and coarsely chop them.

OUTDOOR BARBECUE:
Grill the patties directly over the white charcoal without piercing them with a fork so the juices don't escape. Do not press them down with the spatula— burgers should be juicy and light, not rock-hard hockey pucks. When they bounce like the tip of your nose, they're medium cooked. Place the chopped chilis and a slice of cheese on top and let melt. Then just put it between two pieces of bread and enjoy.

SKILLET:
If you want to cook your burgers in a skillet, that's fine, too. Just use a cast-iron skillet that's so hot it's smoking. Add some oil and flip the burgers every 20 seconds, they'll get juicier that way, until they feel medium cooked.

Serve with ketchup, mustard, and mayonnaise mixed together to make a simple hamburger sauce, as well as thinly sliced white onion.

LEGS OF FIRE

This has to be the best barbecue chicken in the world, because it contains elements from every part of Tex-Mex cuisine's food circle: it's crispy, hot, sweet, fun, and sticky. You can also use wings and thighs for this recipe. Probably breasts, too, but seriously, who would want that?

SERVES 4

2¼–3¼lb/1–1.5kg chicken legs
½ cup/4fl oz/120ml olive oil
1 tablespoon paprika
1 teaspoon chili powder
1 teaspoon cayenne pepper
1 teaspoon garlic powder
1 teaspoon ground white pepper
1 teaspoon dried oregano
1 teaspoon salt
barbecue sauce (see p. 105)

OUTDOOR BARBECUE:
Rub the chicken with the oil and the other dry spices and fry over a direct heat until the juices are running clear.

Drizzle the barbecue sauce over the chicken and finish off on the grill rack until the skin is so crispy that the neighbors complain.

OVEN:
Preheat the oven to 350°F/175°C. Rub the chicken with the oil and the other dry spices and roast in the oven for 30 minutes. Drizzle with the barbecue sauce and turn up the oven to max until everything is nice and crispy.

Serve with guacamole con piña y pepino (see p. 18) and tortilla chips (see p. 13).

BEER CAN CHICKEN

To cook a chicken on a beer can might sound improbable—but the truth is that it's a perfect way to get a flavorful and juicy bird. This is because the beer evaporates inside the chicken, adding both moisture and a nice flavor. Combined with the barbecue's slow and smoky cooking, the end result is simply magnifico.

SERVES 4

1 whole chicken (about 3lb/1.3kg)
corn oil
rendez-vous dry rub (see p. 21)
2 cups/18fl oz/500ml beer

Cook on
indirect heat

For exact method
see p. 34.

Pat the chicken with the oil and the spice mix. Let marinate for 1 hour in the refrigerator. Meanwhile, prepare the barbecue grill for indirect cooking—fill one half with charcoal, in the other half place a pan of water. Drink half of the beer and place the bird on top, with the can in its cavity. Then place the can on the half of the grill that hasn't got any charcoal in it. (Take a look at the photo if you don't get my meaning!) Throw a couple of handfuls of mesquite chips on the coals and close the lid. After 30 minutes, throw in another handful. That should do it for smoke. Let the chicken cook slowly and steadily for 3–4 hours at 230–235°F/110–112°C. The inside temperature of the chicken should be 165–175°F/75–80°C.

Serve with poblano potato salad (see p. 105).

MEMPHIS DRY RIBS

To barbecue really delicious ribs is significantly easier than you might think. However, you do need some patience, along with a six-pack of beer, some music, and a backyard recliner while you're waiting. Dry ribs are spare ribs cooked without barbecue sauce on direct heat but with a spice mix that is massaged into the meat; as a result, they become crispier and chewier than regular sticky ribs.

SERVES 4

4½lb/2kg baby back ribs
¾-1 cup/6-8fl oz/175-240ml
   white wine vinegar
rendez-vous dry rub (see p. 21)

OUTDOOR BARBECUE:
Mix together ¾-1 cup/6-8fl oz/175-240ml of water with the vinegar and a couple of tablespoons of the rub. When the charcoals are white, it's time to start grilling. Dry ribs are grilled over direct heat—with the grill rack straight over the charcoals—and should cook for 1 hour. If it gets too hot, move them over to the indirect side. To avoid burning the ribs, use the vinegar mixture for tenderizing the meat, keeping it juicy and cooling it down. Do it regularly throughout the whole grilling process and make sure it doesn't burn. After 1 hour, sprinkle with more spice mix and serve.

OVEN:
Preheat the oven to 400°F/200°C. Cook for 45-60 minutes. Make sure to turn the ribs over regularly and cool down with the vinegar mixture.

Serve with elotes (see p. 105), and/or guacamole of your choice (see p. 17), and tortilla chips (see p. 13).

TEXAS WET RIBS

Real barbecue ribs are fantastically tasty, tender, and juicy, but contrary to popular belief, they don't melt in your mouth. So don't try to cheat by parboiling the meat—only tacky barbecue joints do that.

SERVES 4

1 tablespoon paprika
1 teaspoon chili powder
1 teaspoon cayenne pepper
1 teaspoon garlic powder
1 teaspoon ground white pepper
1 teaspoon dried oregano
1 teaspoon salt
4¹/₂lb/2kg baby back ribs
3 tablespoons corn oil
barbecue sauce (see p. 105)

Cook on
indirect heat

For exact method
see p. 34.

Serve with elotes (see p. 105),
and/or guacamole of your
choice (see p. 17), and tortilla
chips (see p. 13).

OUTDOOR BARBECUE:
Mix together the dry spices and rub into the meat together with the oil. You could let it marinate for 1 hour (or don't bother). Prepare the barbecue grill by placing charcoal in one half. Don't use too much, the temperature should be 230–250°F/110–120°C. Put the meat in the other half with a pan of water underneath. Throw a couple of handfuls of mesquite wood chips over the coals and close the lid. After 30 minutes, throw another couple of handfuls in. That's enough; 1 hour is all you need so that the meat doesn't get oversmoked. Let the ribs cook on the rack until the meat is tender and juicy: for large ribs, 4–5 hours; for small ones, 3 hours are enough. Add more charcoal when needed and turn the ribs over from time to time. When the meat has turned a nice color and begins falling off the bone—you will need try a bite—it's time to start brushing the ribs with the barbecue sauce and placing the rack directly over the charcoals. Cook on direct heat for a couple of minutes or until the barbecue sauce has caramelized.

OVEN:
Preheat the oven to 225°F/110°C. First, cook in the oven for the same time as above, then cover with barbecue sauce and turn the oven to max until it's caramelized.

BARBECUE SIDES

A human can't live on only barbecued food (unfortunately). So here are a few traditional barbecue sides.

Poblano potato salad
Creamy potato salad with a spicy twist

2¼lb/1kg new potatoes
2–3 tablespoons corn oil
1 whole garlic
2 large fresh poblano chilis or 1 large
   pointed pepper and 1 fresh chili
2 tablespoons mayonnaise
4 scallions
salt
3 tablespoons chopped fresh parsley
3 tablespoons chopped fresh cilantro

Preheat the oven to 400°F/200°C. Coat the potatoes in the oil and roast in the oven until crispy. Put the whole garlic and the chilis or the pepper and chili on the grill until almost black. Remove the skins and blend together with the mayonnaise. Season with salt and mix with the potatoes. Garnish with the parsley and cilantro.

Barbecue sauce
Hot sweet-spicy barbecue sauce

1 brown onion, chopped
6 garlic cloves, finely chopped
1 teaspoon ground cumin
2 tablespoons olive oil
¼ cup/2fl oz/60ml balsamic vinegar
½ cup/3½oz/100g firmly packed
   light brown sugar
¼ cup/2fl oz/60ml Japanese soy sauce
1 tablespoon Worcestershire sauce
½ cup/4fl oz/120ml ketchup
1 tablespoon chili powder

Sauté the onion, garlic, and cumin in oil until the onion is soft. Deglaze the pan with vinegar, add the other ingredients, and boil to a sticky consistency.

Elotes
Mexican grilled corn on the cob

4 fresh ears of corn
2 tablespoons butter, melted
lime wedges
1 cup/8fl oz/240ml crème fraîche
   or sour cream
feta cheese, crumbled, to taste
salt
1 tablespoon chili powder

Soak the ears in water for 15 minutes. Grill for 10 minutes, remove the husks, brush with butter, and grill for another 5 minutes. Squeeze with lime, drizzle with crème fraîche, top with the cheese, then sprinkle with salt and chili powder.

Apple coleslaw
Jazzed-up coleslaw with apple

juice of ½ lime
3 tablespoons mayonnaise
3 tablespoons olive oil
2 tablespoons apple cider vinegar
1 tablespoon poppy seeds
1 green apple
1 large head of red cabbage
salt and freshly ground black pepper

Whisk together the dressing, slice the apple into thin sticks, shred the cabbage, and mix. Season with salt and pepper and let stand for 1 hour.

PART 6

DESSERTS

When it comes to Tex-Mex desserts, it's almost always either one of two things: pies or paletas (homemade ice pops). Luckily, these two also happen to be the two most delicious types of dessert you can make. In this chapter, you'll learn how.

SALTY PECAN APPLE CRUMB PIE

This classic apple pie from Texas could very well be the ultimate dessert. The pecans provide crunch and a nutty flavor, and the salt just makes the sugar even sweeter.

SERVES 6-8

CRUMB TOPPING
2½ cups/9oz/250g pecans
1⅔ cups/7oz/200g all-purpose flour
2 tablespoons packed light brown sugar
2 tablespoons granulated sugar
½ teaspoon salt
½ teaspoon ground cinnamon
7 tablespoons/3½oz/100g butter

APPLE FILLING
4–6 apples
finely grated zest from 1 lemon
½ cup/3½oz/100g granulated sugar
2 tablespoons cornstarch
grated nutmeg

Preheat the oven to 350°F/175°C. Smash the nuts, still in the bag, with a rolling pin or some other hard implement. Process in a food processor together with flour, sugars, salt, cinnamon, and butter until resembling coarse bread crumbs.

Peel and slice the apples and mix together with the other ingredients for the apple filling, then place in an ovenproof dish, about 9½ inches/24cm in diameter.

Sprinkle the crumb topping over the apple filling and bake in the oven for about 40 minutes, until the topping is crunchy and the apples are soft.

Serve with vanilla ice cream, store-bought or homemade (see p. 116).

BOURBON PECAN PIE

Pecan pie is incredibly tasty, so tasty, in fact, that it can be life-threatening. Pecan pie is incredibly unhealthy—with butter and four kinds of sugar (and some liquor). So take a small slice.

SERVES 6-8

PASTRY DOUGH
1 stick/½ cup/4½oz/120g butter, in cubes
2 cups/9oz/250g all-purpose flour
⅓ cup/2oz/50g confectioners' sugar
1 egg

FILLING
3 eggs
¾ cup/5oz/150g granulated sugar
⅓ cup/3½oz/100g dark corn syrup or molasses
1 pinch salt
1 tablespoon vanilla sugar (put a couple of vanilla beans into a jar of superfine sugar, seal well, and let sit for about 2 weeks, or until the sugar takes on the vanilla flavor)
4 tablespoons butter, melted
1 teaspoon ground cinnamon
¼ cup/2fl oz/60ml Bourbon
3 cups/11oz/300g coarsely chopped pecans

Preheat the oven to 350°F/175°C. Mix together the butter, flour, and confectioners' sugar in a bowl. When you've got a crumbly substance, add the egg and 3 tablespoons of water and work together to a dough. Wrap the dough in plastic wrap and let rest in the refrigerator for 20 minutes.

Press the cold dough into a pie pan, about 9½ inches/24cm in diameter, and bake in the oven for about 12 minutes—preferably with some dried rice or beans placed on top of a piece of parchment paper as a weight for a nice and neat result.

Whisk together the eggs, sugar, syrup, salt, and vanilla sugar. Add the melted butter, cinnamon, and Bourbon, and mix.

Place the nuts in the pastry crust, pour the egg mixture over them, and bake in the oven for about 30 minutes. Keep a careful eye on the pie so that it doesn't burn; if it looks like it will, cover with foil. Take out of the oven and let cool.

Serve with vanilla ice cream, store-bought or homemade (see p. 116).

CHOCOLATE MERINGUE PIE

Just the words "chocolate meringue pie" can get dieticians hyperventilating and blood vessels clogging. But scrumptious it is, and you will definitely be remembered if you serve it.

SERVES 6–8

PASTRY DOUGH
1 stick/$\frac{1}{2}$ cup/$4\frac{1}{2}$oz/125g butter, in cubes
3$\frac{1}{4}$ cups/14oz/400g all-purpose flour
$\frac{1}{3}$ cup/2oz/50g confectioners' sugar
1 egg

FILLING
6oz/170g semisweet chocolate
7 tablespoons/$3\frac{1}{2}$oz/100g butter
3 egg yolks
$\frac{1}{4}$ teaspoon salt
$\frac{2}{3}$ cup/125g/$4\frac{1}{2}$oz granulated sugar

MERINGUE
3 egg whites
$\frac{1}{2}$ teaspoon salt
$\frac{1}{3}$ cup/$2\frac{1}{4}$oz/65g superfine sugar

Preheat the oven to 350°F/175°C. Mix together the butter, flour, and confectioners' sugar in a bowl. When you have a crumbly mixture, add the egg and 3 tablespoons of water and work together to a dough. Wrap the dough in plastic wrap and let rest in the refrigerator for 20 minutes.

Press the cold dough into a pie pan and bake in the oven until cooked through for about 15 minutes—preferably with some dried rice or beans placed on top of a piece of parchment paper as a weight for a nice and neat result.

Prepare the chocolate filling by mixing all the ingredients together in a saucepan and then simmering for 10 minutes or until you have a thick mixture.

Whisk the meringue ingredients together in a clean bowl until peaks form, then pour the chocolate mixture into the pastry crust, top with the meringue, and bake in the oven for 5–10 minutes, until the meringue turns a little golden brown.

Tip!

This chocolate pie can be eaten warm, cold, and even frozen like an ice pop.

HELADO DE CAJETA

Cajeta, or dulce de leche, is a kind of Mexican caramel sauce that fits like a glove with homemade vanilla ice cream and toasted coconut. Despite taking some time to cook, this is what I would call a foolproof recipe.

SERVES 6–8

VANILLA ICE CREAM
2 extra-large eggs
1 cup/7oz/200g granulated sugar
1 cup/8fl oz/240ml milk
¼ cup/2fl oz/60ml heavy cream

CAJETA
1 (14-oz/400-g) can sweetened
    condensed milk
2¾ cups/7oz/200g dry unsweetened
    coconut
salt flakes

Start by making the vanilla ice cream. Whisk the eggs until fluffy and add a little of the sugar at a time until it's completely dissolved. Whisk in the milk and cream and pour into an ice-cream maker. If you don't have an ice-cream maker, you can, of course, use store-bought ice cream instead.

Take the can of condensed milk and make two small holes in the lid using a hammer and nail. This is to prevent the can from exploding in your face like a delicate hand grenade. Place the can in a saucepan and fill the pan with water, leaving ¾ inch/2cm of the can above the surface. Bring the water to a boil and let simmer for 3–4 hours, depending on how thick you want the caramel sauce. Top up the water, if necessary.

Take the can out of the water and let cool for a minute or two. Open the can, using a can opener, then pour the caramel sauce into a bowl and whisk to get rid of any lumps.

Toast the dry coconut. Take some ice cream and form into a snowball, roll in the coconut, and drizzle with the caramel sauce. Finish off with a pinch of salt flakes.

PALETAS DE AGUA

Paletas de agua are homemade Mexican ice pops, a little like the ones you can get in supermarkets but fruitier, and they can be made in any flavor you can imagine. So use these as base recipes and start experimenting.

MAKES 10 ice pops per recipe

AVOCADO
2/3 cup/4 1/2 oz/125g granulated sugar
2–3 avocados
2 tablespoons freshly squeezed lime juice
pinch of salt

MANGO
4 ripe mangos
1/2 cup/3 1/2 oz/100g granulated sugar
50ml/2fl oz/scant 1/4 cup freshly squeezed lime juice
cayenne pepper or chili powder (optional)
salt (optional)

STRAWBERRY
2 1/4 lb/1kg fresh strawberries
1 cup/7oz/200g granulated sugar
2 tablespoons freshly squeezed lime juice

YOGURT AND BERRIES
3/4 cup/5oz/150g granulated sugar
1 1/2 cups/12oz/350g Greek yogurt
2 tablespoons honey
3 1/4 cups/14oz/400g fresh raspberries, blueberries, or blackberries

AVOCADO
Bring 1 cup/8fl oz/240ml water and the sugar to a boil and stir until the sugar has dissolved. Let cool. Blend the peeled avocados, sugar syrup, lime juice, and salt together to a smooth mixture.

MANGO
Blend the peeled and diced mangoes, sugar, and lime juice together to a smooth mixture. If you want, you can sprinkle cayenne or chili powder and salt on this variety just before serving.

STRAWBERRIES
Mix together the strawberries and sugar and let rest for 30 minutes, until juicy. Simmer the mixture for 5 minutes and let cool. Blend with 1/2 cup/4fl oz/12ml of water and the lime juice until smooth or leave some chunks.

YOGURT AND BERRIES
Bring 2/3 cup/5fl oz/150ml water and sugar to a boil and stir until the sugar has dissolved. Let cool. Blend the yogurt, sugar syrup, and honey together. Add the berries.

THE POPS
Pour the mixture into an ice-cream maker and churn until it turns to slush. Pour into the ice pop molds. Push down the ice pop stick and freeze for at least 6 hours. You can also skip the ice-cream maker step, but the result will be icier.

PALETAS DE LECHE

Paletas de leche are, like the name suggests, Mexican ice pops made with milk as the base. Keep them in the freezer and take out when you're craving something sweet, or fill a tray with ice and serve a paletas buffet for dessert.

MAKES 10 ice creams per recipe

COCONUT PALETA

2³⁄₄ cups/200g/7oz/dry unsweetened
    coconut
1 vanilla bean
1³⁄₄ cups/14fl oz/400ml coconut milk
1 (14-oz/400-g) can sweetened
    condensed milk
1 cup/8fl oz/220ml light cream
¹⁄₄ teaspoon salt

LIME PALETA

1 (14-oz/400-g) can sweetened
    condensed milk
¹⁄₄ cup/2fl oz/60ml light cream
juice of 4 limes
2 teaspoons finely grated lime zest
salt

COCONUT PALETA

Toast the dry coconut in a dry pan until the flakes have turned a nice brown. Scrape the seeds out of the vanilla bean and add to the coconut milk. Add the rest of the ingredients, including the toasted coconut, and stir. Pour the mixture into an ice-cream maker and churn until you get a soft serve consistency. Pour into the ice pop molds, push down the ice pop sticks, and freeze for at least 6 hours. You can also pour the mixture straight into the molds and skip the ice-cream maker, but the result will be a little icier.

LIME PALETA

Mix all the ingredients together, pour into an ice-cream maker, and churn until you get a soft serving consistency. Pour into ice pop molds, push down the ice pop sticks, and freeze for at least 6 hours. You can also pour the mixture straight into the molds and skip the ice-cream maker, but the result will be a little icier.

When the ice-cream pops are done, just go ahead and experiment with homemade dips and sprinkles of your choice.

Dip suggestions

melted chocolate
toasted coconut
chopped pistachio nuts
crushed mini pretzels
crushed cookies

PART 7

DRINKS

Tex-Mex drinks mean, in most cases, margaritas, beer cocktails, and tequila shots—all of which make you want to get naked and go skinny dipping. But don't get too excited—just start mixing.

MICHELADA

A michelada is a refreshing Mexican beer cocktail that's drunk either when it's hot outside or as hair of the dog. There are many versions of this drink, but it always contains lime, ice, and chili—sometimes tomato juice and even clam juice. Well-cooled glasses are ideal for serving, with or without a salt rim.

MAKES 1 drink

1 lime wedge
salt
ice
1½ cups/12fl oz/350ml Mexican beer
¼ cup/2fl oz/60ml freshly squeezed
   lime juice
½ teaspoon (or more) Tabasco sauce
½ teaspoon Worcestershire sauce

Rub the lime wedge around the edge of a beer glass and dip it into salt.

Fill the glass with ice and pour the beer and lime over it, then drip in as much Tabasco and Worcestershire sauce as you dare.

Lagerita

Since we're looking at mixing beer cocktails, perhaps we should try this one, too? The name lets on how it tastes. Margarita + lager = Lagerita. Ingenious.

Makes 1 drink
ice
¼ cup/2fl oz/50ml
   100% agave tequila
1 tablespoon simple syrup
juice of ½ lime
1½ cups/12fl oz/350ml
   Mexican lager

Fill the glass with ice. Pour in the rest of the ingredients. Drink.

1.

2.

MARGARITA

Although the margarita was invented in Mexico, it's now been completely adopted by United States, where it is a very popular drink. If you want to be more authentically Mexican, you should instead choose to mix a paloma (see p. 131). There are thousands of variations of margarita, but here are a few of my absolute favorites.

1 Mango margarita

The perfect way to start a dinner party is to let the guests have small talk over a table of homemade snacks and one or a couple of deceptively strong mango margaritas. Prepare the ingredients before the guests arrive and then stand ready by the blender to mix the drinks *à la minute*.

Makes 6 drinks

2-3 mangoes
1¼ cups/10fl oz/300ml freshly squeezed lime juice
⅔ cup/5fl oz/150ml freshly squeezed lemon juice
¼ cup/2oz/50g granulated sugar
crushed ice
1 cup/8fl oz/240ml 100% agave tequila
½ cup/3½fl oz/100ml triple sec
salt
lime wedges

Prepare the mango puree by peeling the mangoes and removing the pits. Blend until you've got a lovely puree. Pour into a bowl. Rinse the blender and make the sweet 'n' sour mix by blending the lime juice, lemon juice, and sugar together until the sugar dissolves. Put it in the refrigerator. When it's time to serve, allow 1½ cups/12fl oz/350ml ice, ½ cup/3½fl oz/100ml sweet 'n' sour mix, ½ cup/3½fl oz/100ml mango puree, 3 tablespoons tequila, and 1 tablespoon triple sec per person, and mix together in the blender until frosty. Pour in a glass with salt rim and garnish with 1 lime wedge.

2 Summer margarita

You can have a lot of fun with a cucumber and some liquor, as in this summer fresh margarita with a distinct hint of melon flavor. Very, very fresh.

Makes 8 drinks

¾ cup/5oz/150g granulated sugar
1 tablespoon freshly squeezed lime juice
5 cups/1½lb/700g peeled and diced cucumber
1½ cups/12fl oz/350ml 100% agave tequila
1 cup/8fl oz/240ml freshly squeezed lime juice
ice
salt
cucumber slices

Bring the sugar, ⅔ cup/5fl oz/150ml of water, and the 1 tablespoon of lime juice to a boil to turn into a simple syrup. Let cool. Put the cucumber, tequila, and 1 cup/8fl oz/240ml of the simple syrup into a blender and mix until it's as smooth as possible. Put it in the refrigerator. When it's drinking time, pour ice into a cocktail shaker as well as

$1^1/_2$ cups/12fl oz/350ml of the margarita mixture. Shake for 10–15 seconds and pour into a glass with a salt rim. Garnish with a slice of cucumber.

3 Hibiscus margarita

Dried hibiscus flowers will give your margarita a lovely neon pink color and a tart flower taste. With what's leftover from the hibiscus syrup, you can make a nice drink for the kids.

Makes 6 drinks

1 cup/7oz/200g granulated sugar
2 cups/7oz/200g dried hibiscus flowers
1 lime wedge
2 tablespoons ground cinnamon
2 tablespoons granulated sugar
ice
$1^1/_4$ cups/10fl oz/300ml
**   100% agave tequila**
club soda
lime wedges or cinnamon sticks

Make a sweet 'n' sour mix by simmering $1^3/_4$ cups/14fl oz/400ml of water with the sugar and hibiscus flowers for 30 minutes. Put it in the refrigerator and let soak for at least 2 hours or overnight. When it's time to drink cocktails, rub the lime around the edge of the glass, dip it in a cinnamon-and-sugar blend, and fill it with some ice. Then pour in 3–4 tablespoons of the hibiscus syrup and 3–4 tablespoons of tequila, top it up with some club soda, and decorate with a lime wedge. Or, if you're more sophisticated, a cinnamon stick.

4 Classic margarita

Tex-Mex food is all about having fun and eating and drinking colorful things with a ridiculous amount of flavor. But now and then you come across a wet blanket who complains about your mango margaritas tasting like slushies (yes? and?) and wants a real margarita. If so, make this one. You really can't get more traditional than this.

Makes 1 drink

1 lime wedge
salt
3–4 tablespoons 100% agave tequila, silver or gold
3–4 tablespoons freshly squeezed lime juice
2 tablespoons triple sec
ice

Rub the lime wedge around the glass and dip the glass in the salt. Pour the tequila as well as the lime juice, triple sec, and ice into a cocktail shaker. Shake for a few seconds and pour the strained drink into the glass.

Paloma

The national cocktail of Mexico isn't the margarita but instead the paloma—tequila with grapefruit soda. This is how to make it.

Makes 1 drink

3–4 tablespoons 100% agave tequila
ice
freshly squeezed juice from $1/_2$ lime
grapefruit soda

Fill the glass with ice. Pour in the tequila and squeeze the lime juice over it. Top up with grapefruit soda and sit yourself down to listen to the music on the radio.

SANGRITA

Sangrita means something like "little blood," and this Mexican classic is just that color. The sangrita works like a chaser. You take a sip of tequila, then follow it with a sip of sangrita to let the sweet-sour-hot flavor clean your taste buds.

MAKES 2 drinks

1 cup/8fl oz/240ml tomato juice
1/2 cup/4fl oz/120ml freshly squeezed
   lime juice
1/2 cup/4fl oz/120ml orange juice,
   preferably freshly squeezed
1/2 teaspoon salt
Tabasco or other hot sauce
ice
1/3–1/2 cup/3–4fl oz/90–120ml tequila

Mix everything together except the tequila. Serve by pouring the tequila in one glass and the sangrita in another. Drink.

Mexican sangrita

In traditional Mexican sangrita, pomegranate is often used instead of tomato juice like in the Tex-Mex variety—so you could go ahead and try that, too.

Makes 2 drinks
1/2 cup/4fl oz/120ml
   pomegranate juice
3–4 tablespoons freshly squeezed
   lime juice
1/2 cup/4fl oz/120ml orange juice
Tabasco or other hot sauce
ice

Mix everything together. Drink with tequila.

MEXICAN MOJITO

Who said only Cubans can have fun and whack together mojitos? This Mexican version of the beloved Latino cocktail has a lovely bite of ginger and chili.

MAKES 8 drinks

1³/₄ cups/12oz/350g granulated sugar
1¹/₂ cups/12fl oz/350ml plus
   1 tablespoon freshly squeezed
   lime juice
1 tablespoon finely chopped ginger
¹/₂ habanero chili
1 large bunch of fresh mint
crushed ice
1³/₄ cups/14fl oz/400ml tequila
club soda

Bring the sugar, 1¹/₂ cups/12fl oz/350ml of water, and 1 tablespoon of the lime juice to a boil to make a simple syrup. Add the ginger and habanero (whole) and let cool. Put in the refrigerator.

When it's time to drink, put 8 mint leaves into each glass, pour in 3 tablespoons of the simple syrup, and muddle together (beat the heck out of it) with a stick. Fill the glass with crushed ice, pour 3–4 tablespoons of tequila over the top, add 3 tablespoons lime juice, and top up with some club soda.

AGUA FRESCA

Agua fresca is a kind of Mexican nonalcoholic fruit punch that really breaks the record for thirst-quenching on a hot day. It can be made using pretty much any fruit, and if you want an extra kick, you can slip in some tequila from your hip flask when no one is watching.

SERVES 6-8

3/4 cup plus 1 tablespoon/5³/₄oz/165g
   granulated sugar
1/2 watermelon
freshly squeezed juice of 4 limes
ice
5 cups/9oz/250g fresh mint
4 cups/1³/₄ pints/1 liter club soda

Make a simple syrup by bringing 1/2 cup/3¹/₂fl oz/100ml of water and the sugar to a boil. Let cool.

Blend the melon in a blender or food processor, preferably without any seeds, add the simple syrup and lime juice, and pour into a large punch bowl along with some ice and the mint and club soda.

For the over-21s version, you can add tequila.

Agua de piña

Because pineapple is naturally acidic, this agua fresca doesn't need any lime. If you want to be a little fancy, on the other hand, serve it out of a genuine Mexican punch bowl—a so-called "vitrolero."

Serves 6-8
1 fresh pineapple
1¹/₄ cups/9oz/250g granulated sugar
ice

Mix the pineapple with 8¹/₂ cups/ 3¹/₂ pints/2 liters water and the sugar in a blender or food processor. Strain to get rid of the pulp and pour into an ice-filled pitcher.

TEX-MEX PICKLEBACK

A pickleback is a shot of whiskey that is immediately followed by a shot of pickle juice—any kind will do. The way it works is that the sour-sweet pickle juice neutralizes the alcohol flavor and quenches the gag reflex. Plus, it's a little revolting and tasty at the same time and makes you want to challenge the biggest person in the room to arm wrestle. The Tex-Mex version uses Bourbon.

MAKES 1 shot

3–4 tablespoons pickle juice, any kind will do
3–4 tablespoons good Bourbon

Pour the pickle juice into a shot glass and the Bourbon in another. Then drink the whiskey first, all of it in one go you wuss, with the shot of pickle juice to follow directly afterward.

Habanero tequila

If you want a little more bite in your tequila, you can always flavor it with different herbs, spices, and fruits. This method, however, is classic.

Makes 1 bottle
3 habanero chilis
3 cups/1¼ pints/750ml 100% agave tequila

Seed the fresh chilis. Take a sip of tequila so that the chilis fit and then push them down into the bottle. Let sit for 3 days, then strain through a strainer.

INDEX

STERLING EPICURE
New York

An Imprint of Sterling Publishing
1166 Avenue of the Americas
New York, NY 10036

Sterling Epicure edition first published 2015

Published in Great Britain in 2013 by Pavilion Books Company Limited
First published in Sweden in 2012 as *Texmex från grunden* by Natur & Kultur, Stockholm

Text © 2012 by Jonas Cramby
Photography © 2012 by Roland Persson, except photos on pp. 5, 6, 8-9, 32-33, 36-37, 46-47, 60-61, 68-69, 82-83,
88-89, 110-111, 126-127 © 2012 by Jonas Cramby

ISBN: 978-1-4549-1629-1

Distributed in Canada by Sterling Publishing
c/o Canadian Manda Group, 664 Annette Street
Toronto, Ontario, Canada M6S 2C8

For information about custom editions, special sales, and premium
and corporate purchases, please contact Sterling Special Sales at 800-805-5489 or
specialsales@sterlingpublishing.com.

Manufactured in China

2 4 6 8 10 9 7 5 3 1

www.sterlingpublishing.com